D1448149

Awesome Facts

about

Earthquakes

This edition published in 2001
© Aladdin Books Ltd 1999
Produced by
Aladdin Books Ltd
28 Percy Street
London W1P 0LD

ISBN 0-7496-4246-7 (paperback)

Previously published in hardcover
in the series "I Didn't Know That"
ISBN 0-7496-3407-3 (hardback)

First published in Great Britain in 1999 by
Aladdin Books/Watts Books
96 Leonard Street
London EC2A 4XD

Editor: Liz White
Design: David West Childen's Books
Designer: Flick Killerby
Illustrators: Peter Roberts - Allied Artists,
Jo Moore, Graham Kennedy - Allied Artists

Printed in the U.A.E

All rights reserved
A CIP catalogue record for this book is available from
the British Library

Awesome Facts about

Earthquakes

Clare Oliver

Aladdin / Watts
London • Sydney

Don't forget to check the borders for extra amazing facts.

CAVAN COUNTY LIBRARY
ACC No. C/140550
CLASS NO. J551.22
INVOICE NO. S453 Global Learning
PRICE €9-50
7 7 NOV 2003

Contents

Introduction

Did *you* know that there are over a million earthquakes every year? ... that roads and bridges can be snapped in two? ... that earthquakes under the sea cause tidal waves?

Discover for yourself amazing facts about earthquakes and the devastation they can cause. Learn how to predict them and find out what to do if you get caught in one.

Look out for this symbol which means there is a fun project for you to try.

Is it true or is it false? Watch for this symbol and try to answer the question before reading on for the answer.

The longest-ever recorded quake lasted four minutes in Alaska in 1964. The ocean bed was shaken up and down, causing a 10-metre-high wall of water to hit the coast.

Earth splitters

The ground beneath your feet may feel firm, but it's not! Sometimes strains build up under the surface, the ground rumbles and the solid rock cracks apart. This is called a tremor or, if it's big, an earthquake.

A big quake struck Afghanistan in 1998. Many people's remote homes were destroyed so they had to resettle elsewhere.

 True or false? An earthquake at night is called a moonquake.

Answer: **False**

A moonquake is a tremor on the moon. Sometimes bits of space rock, called *meteorites*, smash into the moon and make the ground shake.

There are over a million earthquakes every year; some are tiny.

Making waves

There are waves of energy which travel through the ground. The Earth's surface is covered in *plates* which constantly push against each other. When the plates move apart shock waves are sent through the land. You can't see shock waves but you can feel them.

Most earthquakes happen along *fault* lines where the rocks are weak and where two or more plates meet.

SEARCH & FIND

Can you find four cars?

FIND & SEARCH

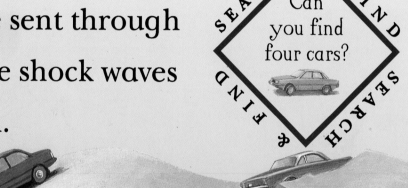

The shock waves start deep underground, at the *focus* of the pressure between the plates. The place where these waves hit the surface will be the earthquake's centre, which scientists call the *epicentre*.

Epicentre

Fault

Focus

Plates start to move

Quake occurs

The pressure can build up for centuries, but eventually – snap! – the plates shift. The pressure escapes in the form of shock waves that ripple outwards from the quake's focus.

See what happens when one of the Earth's plates shifts. For the Earth's plate, use a rug. Add some buildings: small boxes will do. Pull one end of the rug sharply to move the 'plate'. What happens to the boxes?

A quake's first shock waves are called body waves.

On the San Andreas Fault, in California, USA, beams of laser light shine across the fault. If a section of earth slips a tiny bit, detectors on the other side measure the slippage.

Quake detectors

Early warnings are very valuable in quake zones. This bronze pot (right) was the first quake detector. In a tremor, a dragon would drop its ball into a toad's mouth. By seeing which toad held a ball, the inventor knew where the quake was starting.

A *seismograph* (right) records the ground vibrations. The line is straight until the earth shakes. The bigger the zigzags, the larger the quake.

True or false?
A *creepmeter* measures the length of the slimy trail a snail makes.

Answer: **False**

It is an underground machine that measures how much the Earth's plates shift, or creep.

There is a mini earthquake in Greece every three days.

Measuring quakes

Scientists number earthquakes to show their strength. The Richter scale grades the strength of an earthquake from 0-9 using seismograph readings. A quake that makes a church bell ring is grade 4 on the Richter scale.

The *Mercalli scale* (right) grades quakes from I (one) to XII (twelve). A grade IV (four) quake causes the same sort of shaking as a heavy truck passing.

1. EARTHQUAKE FELT BY INSTRUMENTS AND ONLY A FEW PEOPLE.

4. FELT INDOORS LIKE PASSING OF HEAVY TRUCKS. DISHES AND WINDOWS RATTLE.

7. FELT BY DRIVERS. WAVES ON PONDS. DIFFICULT TO STAND.

8. MONUMENTS AND CHIMNEYS COLLAPSE.

11. FEW BUILDINGS LEFT STANDING. BRIDGES AND UNDERGROUND PIPES DESTROYED. CRACKS IN THE GROUND.

Mercalli based his scale on what quake victims reported.

KU-141-280

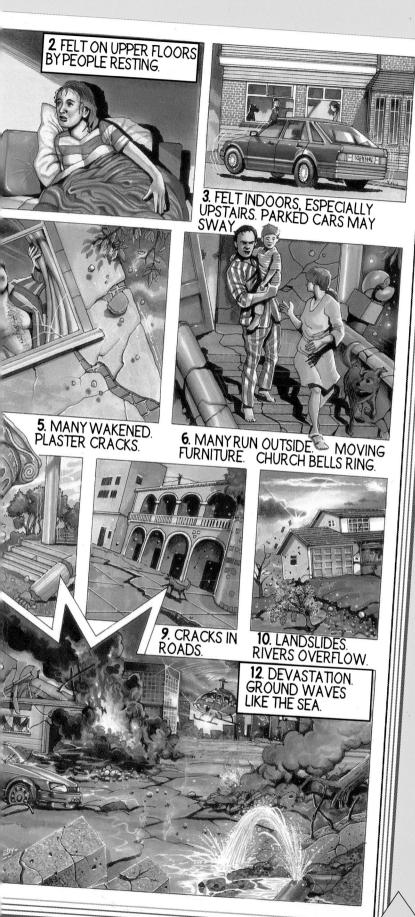

2 FELT ON UPPER FLOORS BY PEOPLE RESTING.

3. FELT INDOORS, ESPECIALLY UPSTAIRS. PARKED CARS MAY SWAY.

5. MANY WAKENED. PLASTER CRACKS.

6. MANY RUN OUTSIDE. MOVING FURNITURE. CHURCH BELLS RING.

9. CRACKS IN ROADS.

10. LANDSLIDES. RIVERS OVERFLOW.

12. DEVASTATION. GROUND WAVES LIKE THE SEA.

True or false?
Soldiers marching in step can topple a bridge.

Answer: **True**

Soldiers break step when crossing small bridges. If they marched in step, the bridge might bounce and break! Many bridges shake, topple and break under a quake's pressure.

SEARCH & FIND · FIND & SEARCH · FIND & SEARCH ·

Can you find four dogs?

Bridge breakers

Earthquakes can cause enormous damage. When a big quake struck Northridge, California, in 1994, three roads were closed as ten supporting bridges collapsed. The quake measured between VIII (eight) and IX (nine) on the Mercalli scale.

Quakes that hit cities cause most damage, as expensive bridges, roads and buildings must be rebuilt. In 1995, a quake shifted the city of Kobe in Japan 1.7 m. Six hundred metres of motorway toppled sideways.

 The Northridge quake was the costliest U.S. natural disaster ever.

The Kobe quake toppled a fish-shaped restaurant.

A powerful earthquake can twist solid metal train tracks as if they were pipe cleaners. This happened in Kobe, Japan, in 1995.

SEARCH & FIND

Can you find the missing road section?

15

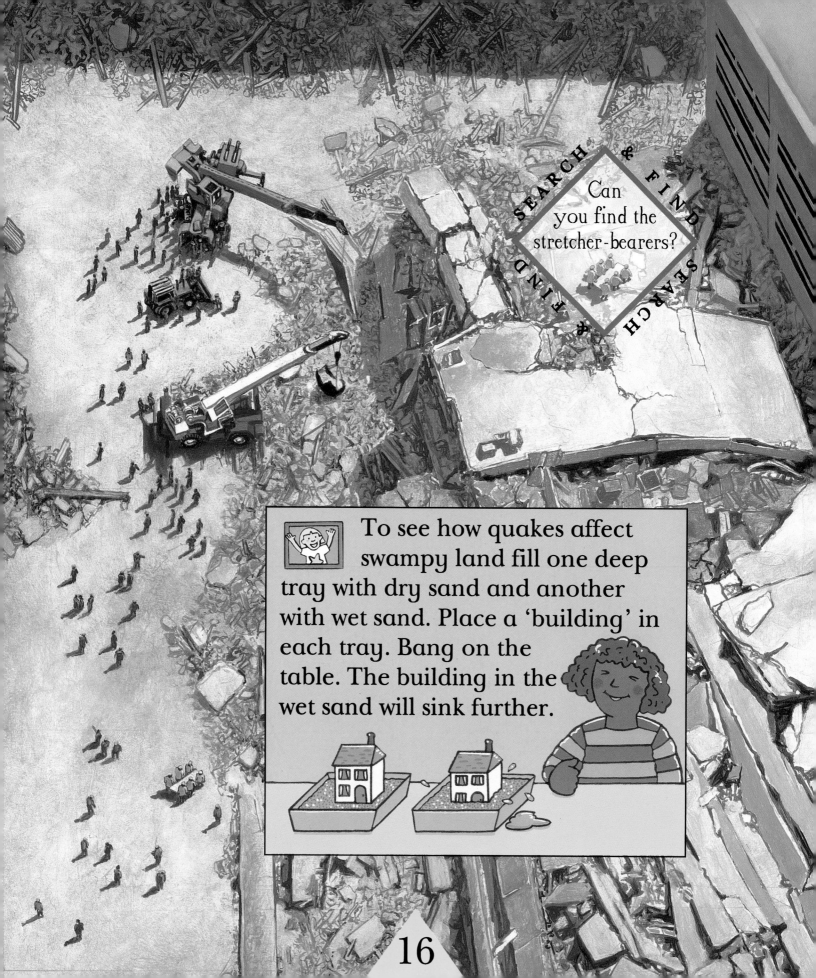

SEARCH & FIND & SEARCH & FIND & SEARCH & FIND &

Can you find the stretcher-bearers?

To see how quakes affect swampy land fill one deep tray with dry sand and another with wet sand. Place a 'building' in each tray. Bang on the table. The building in the wet sand will sink further.

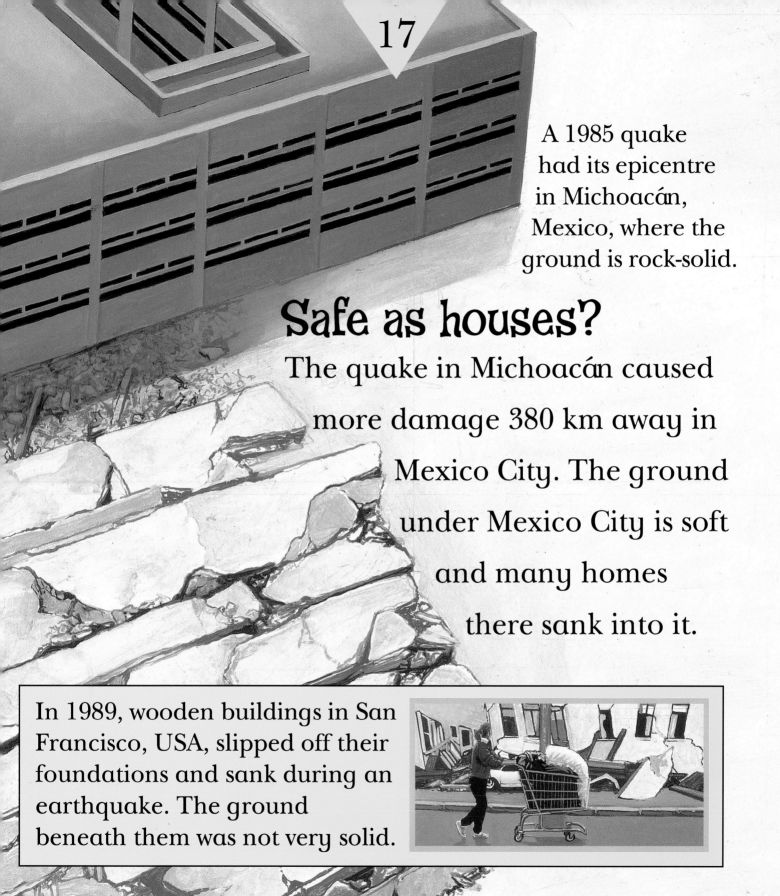

A 1985 quake had its epicentre in Michoacán, Mexico, where the ground is rock-solid.

Safe as houses?

The quake in Michoacán caused more damage 380 km away in Mexico City. The ground under Mexico City is soft and many homes there sank into it.

In 1989, wooden buildings in San Francisco, USA, slipped off their foundations and sank during an earthquake. The ground beneath them was not very solid.

Mexico City is built on a dried-up, swampy lake.

True or false?
Before a quake,
ponds get extra smelly.

Answer: **True**

As the pressure under the ground
builds up, gases build up too and leak
into ground-water, which is the water
just below land-level, and pond-water.
Some of these gases smell.

Animals can become
jumpy just before
a quake. It's as
if they know
what is about
to happen.

Life-saving tables

One of the biggest quake dangers is being hit on the head. Find something to protect your head, then crouch under a sturdy table. Another safe place to stand is in a doorway.

The film *Earthquake* told the story of a big tremor hitting Los Angeles in the USA. Everyone who lives there in real life has to be prepared in case a 'Big One' strikes.

Gases in the ground often make quake fires so hot that they can melt glass.

In 1970, an earthquake caused one of the worst landslides ever. The shock waves dislodged ice on the Andes, which turned into a *mudflow* that swept away the town of Yungay, Peru, killing 50,000.

SEARCH & FIND & SEARCH & FIND

Can you find three rooftops?

The Yungay landslide was 80 metres high.

! A mudflow can pick up enough power to uproot a tree.

True or false?
Earthquakes make mud boil.

Answer: **True**
A quake's shock waves can make mud spurt up in 30-cm cones, or *sand boils*.

Muddy menace

Sometimes, the after-effects of an earthquake are more dangerous than the quake itself. When a quake shakes ice from mountain peaks, the ice melts and runs downwards. As it flows it gathers pieces of earth and rock. The mudflow can move fast enough to sweep away people, cars and houses.

Wave of destruction

Even offshore quakes can cause real damage. When an earthquake strikes at sea, the trembling sea bed churns up monster waves. In 1755, a quake 322 km out to sea from Lisbon, Portugal, created a huge tidal wave that destroyed the city's buildings.

SEARCH & FIND Can you find the donkey? *FIND & SEARCH*

True or false?
A tidal wave is called a *tsunami*.

Answer: **True**
'Tsunami' is the proper word to use. It's a Japanese word that means 'harbour wave'. Japan gets hit by many tsunamis from the Pacific.

In 1992, an earthquake rumbled out at sea off the coast of Nicaragua, Central America. The quake made 15-m-high waves – over ten times as tall as you – and wrecked 300 km of coast.

True or false?
Eight elephants hold up the world.

Answer: **True**

True, if you believe the ancient Hindu myth that the Earth rests on eight elephants. When an elephant shakes its head, there is an earthquake.

! The Greeks thought the god Poseidon banged the sea bed to cause quakes.

The ancient Greeks believed a huge bull lived under the palace at Knossos, Crete, and that its bellowing shook the Earth. Knossos was flattened by a quake 3,400 years ago.

Earthquake legends

Many cultures have myths about earthquakes. Legend has it that in 1855, when the gods had left Tokyo to visit a distant shrine, a catfish called the Namazo thrashed about. With no gods to protect it, the city suffered a bad quake.

25

After an earthquake, rescue workers need special equipment for finding trapped victims. *Infra-red cameras* can 'see' body heat through many layers of rubble. With the help of these, rescuers know where to start digging first.

SEARCH & FIND Can you find three rescue dogs? FIND & SEARCH

Japan has an annual National Disaster Prevention Day on the anniversary of the 1923 Tokyo earthquake. People practise what to do in a quake. Children wear fire-proof capes (right).

26

Rescue methods

Buried quake survivors must be found quickly. Sniffer dogs are used to search for victims. They are specially trained for the job. With their sensitive noses, the dogs can smell where people are lying beneath rubble.

True or false?

The worst quake last century killed 750,000 people.

Answer: **Don't know**
Some say 750,000 died at Tangshan, China, in 1976. But the official figure is just under 250,000.

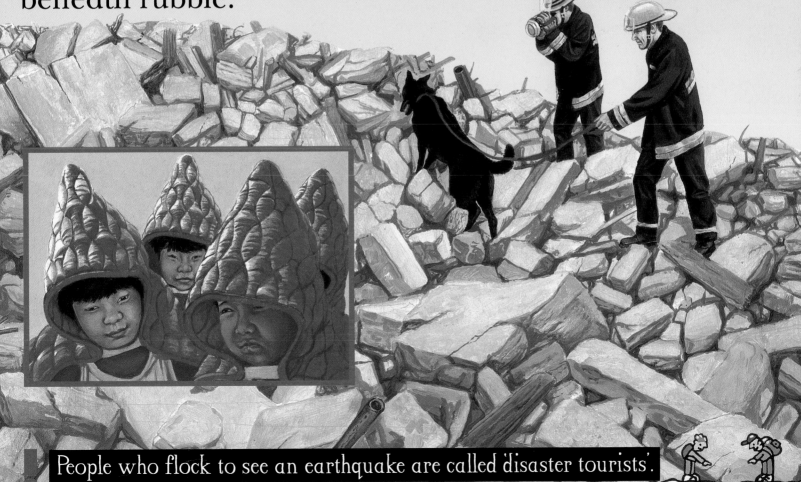

People who flock to see an earthquake are called 'disaster tourists'.

True or false?

Houses were made of paper.

Answer: True
In Japan some houses were built of paper and balsa wood: easy and cheap to rebuild!

Quake-proof

Some buildings are specially built to survive earthquakes. San Francisco's Transamerica Building is wider at the bottom than at the top, and so has a sturdier base to withstand tremors.

Use building blocks to test how sturdy different shapes are when you make the table shake. A shape that is wider at the top than at the bottom is the most unstable.

Japanese pagodas are brilliant at withstanding quakes. Only two pagodas have collapsed from quakes in the last 1,400 years.

Glossary

Creepmeter
A machine that measures 'creep', that is, how far each year the Earth's plates move.

Epicentre
The centre of an earthquake on the ground.

Fault
A crack in the rocks that form the Earth's surface.

Focus
The starting-point of an earthquake underground.

Infra-red camera
A camera that shows up any hot areas, for example body heat, as red. It can see right 'through' darkness or rubble.

Mercalli scale
A range of numbers that describes how powerful an earthquake is, based on what witnesses of the quake saw.

Meteorite
Space rock that has broken away from a comet's fiery tail and smashes into a planet or moon.

Mudflow

A 'river' of rock, earth and water that can start out when an ice-covered mountain peak is shaken and melted in an earthquake.

Seismograph

A machine that measures the force of an earthquake. A print-out from the machine is called a seismogram.

Plates

Large sections of the Earth's crust which are constantly moving against each other.

Tsunami

A giant wave, caused by an earthquake or a volcanic eruption.

Sand boil

Cone-shaped peaks of bubbling mud, created by earthquakes.

Index